2/00

IN SEARCH OF THE AMAZING
DINOSAURS
A journey through time

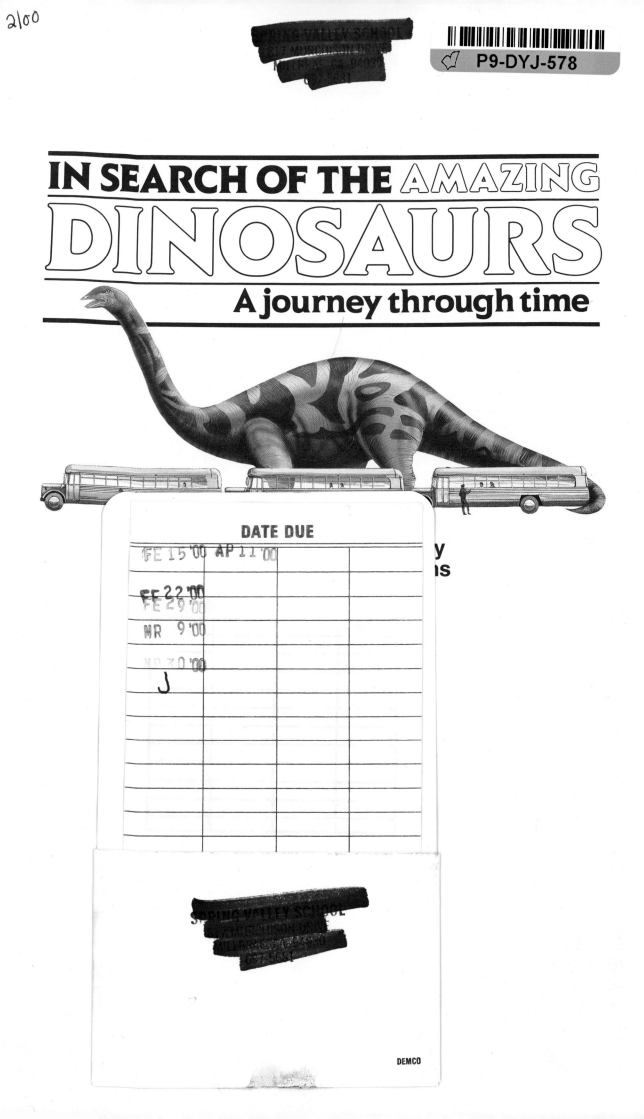

GIANTS AMONG GIANTS

If we could go back in time 180 million years ago on a prehistoric safari, we would find ourselves in the world of the dinosaurs. Our camper would be dwarfed by these giants, the largest of which were the plant-eating dinosaurs (herbivores). These dinosaurs, the largest creatures ever to exist on this planet, roamed in large herds through the prehistoric forests of evergreens and palm trees. Most had long necks to enable them to reach the tender shoots of trees, and long tails for balance.

APATOSAURUS

STEGOSAURUS

Compare the size of the prehistoric reptiles to the size of a camper.

The biggest of all

One of the heaviest dinosaurs of all was **Brachiosaurus** which weighed up to 85 tons — as much as 13 adult African elephants. At 39 feet it was also one of the tallest.

A few years ago, the bones of an even larger dinosaur were found. Named Ultrasaurus, the weight of this supergiant has been estimated at over 130 tons.

APATOSAURUS

BRACHIOSAURUS

The longest dinosaur

Diplodocus stretched over 86 feet from the tip of its tail to the blunt snout of its tiny head. It was as long as three school buses placed end to end, and could easily look over a two-story building.

Dinosaur footprints

Sets of fossilized dinosaur footprints have been found by archaeologists. They were formed in soft sand or mud as the huge reptiles crossed prehistoric rivers or lakes.

As the ground hardened, layers of dirt or dust covered them and they turned to stone. One **Apatosaurus** footprint has been discovered that is large enough to hold over 17 gallons of water.

DIPLODOCUS

Compare Diplodocus, the longest dinosaur, to three school buses placed end to end.

A living radiator

One of the strangest looking dinosaurs lived during the Jurassic Period (180-135 million years ago). **Stegosaurus** was 23 feet long and weighed about 6 tons. It was easily distinguished from other giant herbivores by the double row of bony plates along its back.

Dinosaurs were cold-blooded and needed the sun's heat to be active. The Stegosaurus was able to control its body temperature by using its plates. When it grew too hot, the Stegosaurus would turn away from the sun to lose body heat through the plates. When it was too cold, it let the warming sun heat the blood passing through the plates. This allowed it to be active for longer periods than other dinosaurs.

Spiked thumbs

Iguanodon was a 32-foot plant eater that lived over much of the earth. More Iguanodon skeletons have been found than those of any other dinosaur.

Its "hand" had five fingers. The middle three were like hoofs, suggesting that it sometimes moved on all fours. A fourth finger was flexible and may have been used for grasping. The fifth finger, or thumb, was a sharp bony spike that may have served as a weapon.

Giant bodies, tiny brains

Despite their enormous size, the giant plant eaters had very small brains that were seldom larger than an apple. The equivalent in a human would be a brain about a quarter of an inch long. It would have taken a long time for messages to reach the brain, and therefore most of the big dinosaurs had extra control centers called "intumescences" in their nervous systems. These extra "brains" helped the dinosaurs move their large hind legs and long tails.

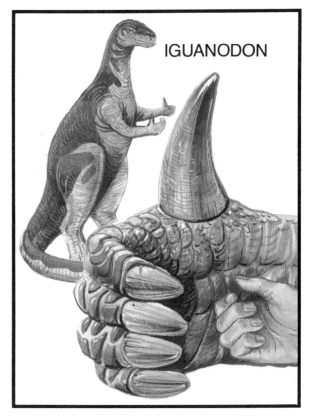

IGUANODON

HUMAN BRAIN

DIPLODOCUS BRAIN

APPLE

INTUMESCENCE

INTUMESCENCE

The crested dinosaurs

Over 100 million years ago, even stranger large reptiles evolved. The Hadrosaurs, or "duck-billed" dinosaurs, had scooped jaws for feeding in marshes or swamps. Many of these creatures had peculiar crests on their heads.

Corythosaurus had a long, narrow, disc-like crest. The 40–foot Parasaurolophus had a hollow crest over 6 feet long. Scientists believe the crests may have improved these dinosaurs' hearing or amplified their voices when seeking a mate or trying to scare away enemies.

Pachycephalosaurs had skulls 10 inches thick which they used as battering rams.

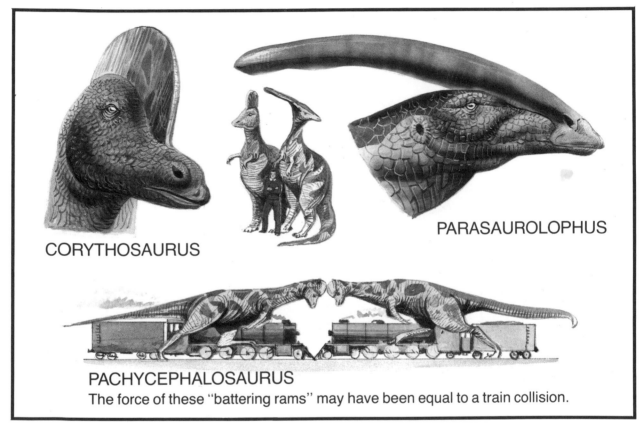

CORYTHOSAURUS

PARASAUROLOPHUS

PACHYCEPHALOSAURUS
The force of these "battering rams" may have been equal to a train collision.

A dinosaur nest

Like most reptiles today, dinosaurs produced their young as eggs. Many species laid their eggs in shallow nests which they often covered over so that the warm sand would incubate them. Others guarded open nests and tended the young when they hatched.

YOUNG PROTOCERATOPS HATCHING

HEN'S EGG

If it was possible to go back 135 million years into the past, it would probably be safer to travel by boat once you arrived. This was the time when the fiercest hunters ever known lived on the earth. They were a new breed of dinosaur that walked on their hind legs. This gave them extra speed and agility. Armed with powerful jaws and dagger-like teeth, they prowled through the warm, moist forests where the first flowering plants were beginning to appear.

These fierce dinosaurs were meat eaters (carnivores), and preyed on the plant-eating dinosaurs that also roamed the earth at this time. These plant eaters evolved various ways of protecting themselves from their enemies. Some grew heavy bony armor or dangerous spikes. Others stayed near the water or in marshes where they could flee to safety, or lived and traveled in packs to outnumber their foes.

STEGOSAURUS

TRICERATOPS

Although there were no boats or people in prehistoric times, compare them to the size of the battling dinosaurs.

PTERANODON

TYRANNOSAURUS

POLACANTHUS

SPRING VALLEY SCHOOL
817 MURCHISON DRIVE
MILLBRAE, CA 94030
697-5681

COELOPHYSIS

Swift hunter

Coelophysis was one of
the first hunters to move on
its hind legs for greater speed
and agility. Coelophysis was
10 feet long and its slim body and hollow
bones allowed it to run as fast as
someone riding a bicycle.

DEINONYCHUS CLAW

TIGER CLAW

The deadly claw

The **Deinonychus** was between 10 and
12 feet long and stood 5 feet tall.
Deinonychus attacked in packs, using its
sharp hind claws to slash at its prey.

These talons were even deadlier than
those of today's tiger and folded back as
Deinonychus raced towards its victim.
Grasping its prey with its front claws, it
would lash out with its hind legs, flicking
the huge talons forward like scythes.

DEINONYCHUS

TIGER

Living tanks

The **ankylosaurs** were slow, clumsy plant eaters. Their backs and sides were covered in thick bony armor and some, like **Polacanthus**, had long spikes projecting from their bodies. As well as its spiky armor, **Scolosaurus** carried two bone spears on its tail for defense.

The **Ankylosaurus** was truly a living tank. It grew up to 35 feet long and weighed about 3 tons. Its tail ended in a huge bony lump which served as a club against its attackers.

Dinosaur teeth

Meat-eating dinosaurs such as **Megalosaurus** had long sharp teeth to hold and kill their prey. Compare these to the teeth of the plant-eating **Iguanodon** and **Stegosaurus** that had teeth shaped to cut through tough plant stems. **Hadrosaurs** had up to 2000 teeth to grind up marsh plants.

MEGALOSAURUS

HUMAN

LION

IGUANODON

STEGOSAURUS

HADROSAUR JAW

POLACANTHUS

SCOLOSAURUS

ANKYLOSAURUS

Compare the size of Ankylosaurus to the size of an Army tank.

King of the dinosaurs

Tyrannosaurus was the most fearsome hunter ever known. Weighing up to 7 tons, this giant hunter was nearly 50 feet long and was as tall as many two-story buildings. Its powerful head was almost 5 feet long with jaws that opened wide enough to swallow a man in one gulp.

Although the teeth of a Tyrannosaurus were over 7 inches long, its forelimbs were almost useless. The arms were too short even to reach its own mouth and because scientists believe Tyrannosaurus slept on its belly, they could only have been used to help it stand up.

TYRANNOSAURUS

Compare the size of the Tyrannosaurus to a two-story house you might see in your neighborhood.

Dangerous prey

One of the few dinosaurs that was a match for Tyrannosaurus was the huge **Triceratops**. This 5 ton, 30 foot long plant eater used its three large horns as lances, and had a massive bone headshield. Other members of the ceratops family had different horn arrangements. **Monoclonius** had a single horn while **Styracosaurus** had several.

The smallest dinosaur

One of the smallest dinosaur hunters discovered was **Compsognathus**. This lightly built, fast-running meat eater was not much larger than a chicken and lived on a diet of small lizards.

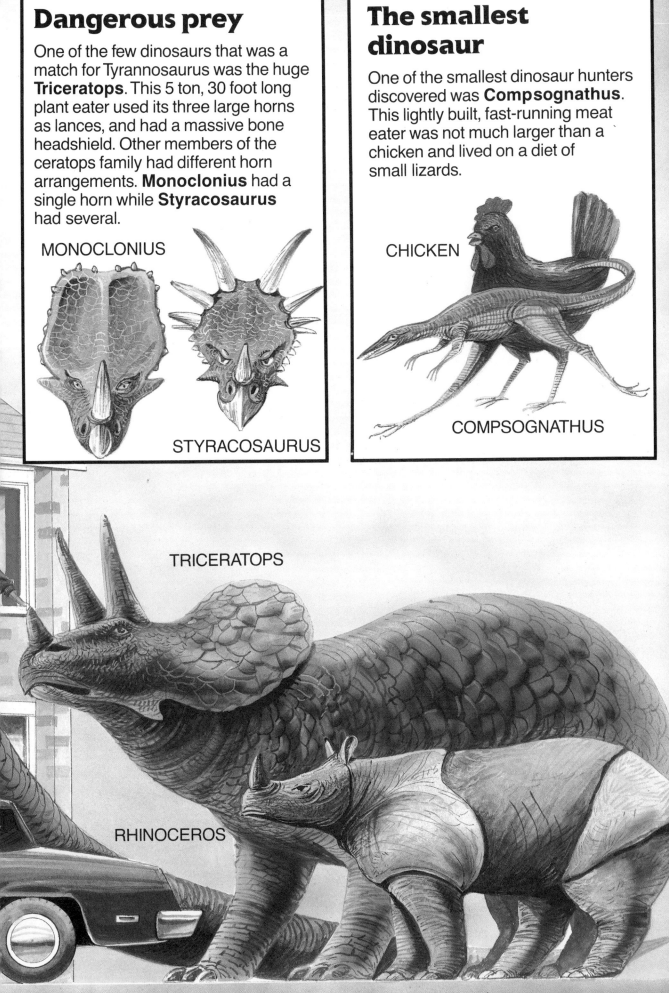

MONOCLONIUS

STYRACOSAURUS

CHICKEN

COMPSOGNATHUS

TRICERATOPS

RHINOCEROS

Compare the size of the Triceratops to a rhinoceros that you might see in a zoo.

DINOSAURS OF SEA AND AIR

While the fierce dinosaur hunters ruled the land, some reptiles returned to the seas from which they had evolved millions of years earlier. Others learned to fly to escape their enemies and to find new sources of food. It would be very exciting to travel through these prehistoric seas if we could take a submarine back through time to see the huge monsters that hunted there.

RHAMPHORYNCHUS

PTERANODON

KRONOSAURUS

ICHTHYOSAURUS

ARCHELON

Compare the size of the prehistoric sea-dwelling reptiles to the scuba diver.

A modern hang-glider would be dwarfed by some of the extraordinary flying reptiles of this period. The first winged dinosaurs were small, clumsy gliders, but as time passed they grew larger and stronger, swooping from the cliffs to snatch fish from the waves below. One species was even bigger than many of today's light aircraft.

Some of the large flying reptiles from prehistoric times were larger than airplanes flying today.

PLESIOSAURUS

A voyage in a modern mini submarine would be very exciting if you could take one back through time.

DINICHTHYS

ep

med the land
giants. The

A water-skier would be dwarfed in comparison to the size of the prehistoric giants of the sea.

ELASMOSAURUS

ICHTHYOSAURUS

Ancient dolphins

Some dinosaurs looked very
much like animals living today.
Ichthyosaurs, which grew from
3 to 30 feet in length, had sleek
shapes, flippers and fish-like
tails like today's dolphins.

Submarine hunters

Kronosaurus was one of the fiercest of the short-necked
plesiosaurs. Its 12 – foot jaws were lined with teeth
and not even the enormous turtle Archelon,
with a shell up to 13 feet across,
was safe from this hunter.

DOLPHIN

KRONOSAURUS

Giant shells

Ammonites were coiled shells up to
6 feet in diameter, as big as a man.
Trilobites had jointed shells up to
2 feet long.

TRILOBITE   AMMONITE

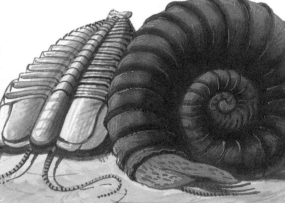

Winged lizards

The first flying reptiles appeared about 200 million years ago. Their wings were leathery flaps of skin stretching from their sides to each of their four limbs. They could glide well, but found it hard to fly. Plesiosaur fossils show that many of these winged reptiles were caught and eaten as they flapped awkwardly over the water.

Crested flyer

Pteranodons were one of the larger flying reptiles with a wingspan of up to 22 feet but a body no larger than a turkey. A large bony crest helped balance the long toothless jaws and may have acted like a simple rudder.

Airborne giant

The largest creature ever to take to the air was **Quetzalcoatlus**, a huge flying monster with an enormous wingspan. From wingtip to wingtip it measured up to 48 feet – 10 feet wider than a Phantom jet fighter.

PTERANODON

Tail rudder

An early pterosaur was **Rhamphorynchus** which was about the size of an eagle. Unlike later relatives, it had teeth which pointed forward to spear fish, and a long tail ending in a paddle-shaped disc to steer with. Some fossil evidence suggests that it was covered with hair which could mean that it was warm-blooded.

QUETZALCOATLUS

Compare the size of this Phantom fighter and the hang glider to these flying giants.

Half bird, half reptile

Archaeopteryx is one of the most puzzling prehistoric creatures. About the size of a crow, it had a lizard's skeleton, teeth, a bone tail and claws on its front limbs. But it also had wings, a bird's skull, wishbone, and eyes and was covered in feathers. It lacked the muscles to fly like a modern bird and could only glide.

One way flyers

Early pterosaurs could only glide and had to crawl back to higher ground.

WHERE DINOSAURS LIVED

The map below shows where fossil evidence of the dinosaurs discussed in this book has been discovered.

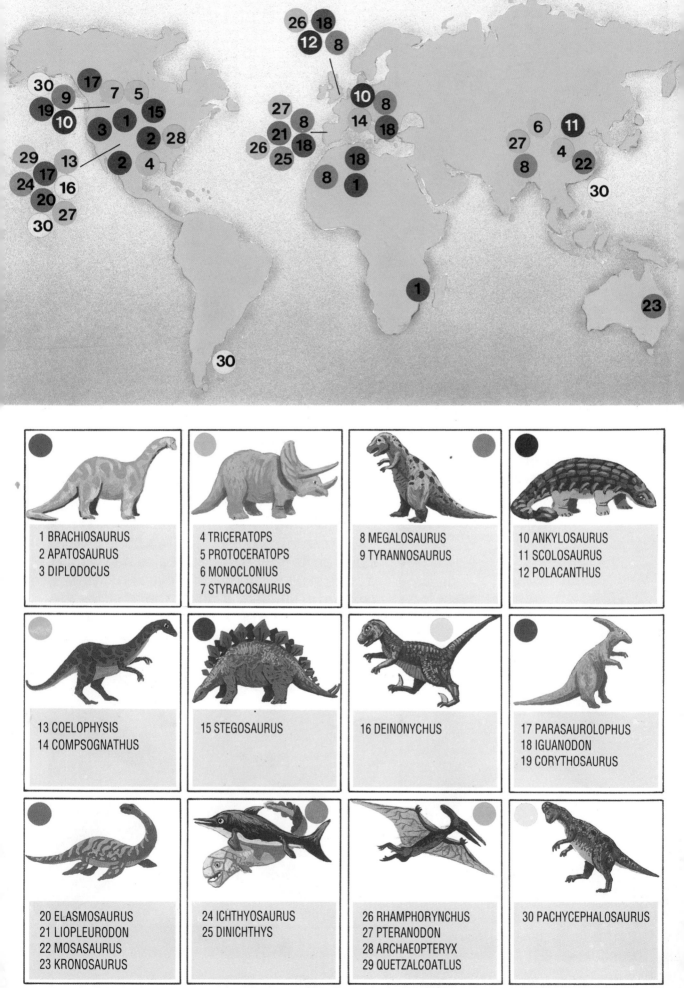

1 BRACHIOSAURUS
2 APATOSAURUS
3 DIPLODOCUS

4 TRICERATOPS
5 PROTOCERATOPS
6 MONOCLONIUS
7 STYRACOSAURUS

8 MEGALOSAURUS
9 TYRANNOSAURUS

10 ANKYLOSAURUS
11 SCOLOSAURUS
12 POLACANTHUS

13 COELOPHYSIS
14 COMPSOGNATHUS

15 STEGOSAURUS

16 DEINONYCHUS

17 PARASAUROLOPHUS
18 IGUANODON
19 CORYTHOSAURUS

20 ELASMOSAURUS
21 LIOPLEURODON
22 MOSASAURUS
23 KRONOSAURUS

24 ICHTHYOSAURUS
25 DINICHTHYS

26 RHAMPHORYNCHUS
27 PTERANODON
28 ARCHAEOPTERYX
29 QUETZALCOATLUS

30 PACHYCEPHALOSAURUS